SUPER SCIENTISTS

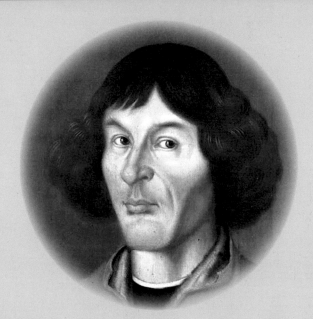

NICOLAUS COPERNICUS

Sarah Ridley

W
FRANKLIN WATTS
LONDON • SYDNEY

First published in 2014
by Franklin Watts

Copyright © Franklin Watts 2014

Franklin Watts
338 Euston Road
London NW1 3BH

Franklin Watts Australia
Level 17/207 Kent Street
Sydney, NSW 2000

Editor in Chief: John C. Miles
Design: Jonathan Hair and Matt Lilly
Art Director: Peter Scoulding
Picture Research: Diana Morris
Original design concept: Sophie Williams

Picture credits: Blueminiu/Dreamstime: 23. The British
Library Board: 13. Endaemon/Dreamstime: 8. Forum/UIG/
Bridgeman Images: 19. Interfoto/Alamy: 18. Interfoto/
Superstock: 6. Christos Kotsiopoulos: 10-11. Museum of
Jagiellonian University: front cover cbg. Neirfy/Shutterstock:
4. Nihil Novi/CC/Wikipedia: 5. Sheila Terry/SPL: 7, 22.
Mieczyslaw Wielczko/Alamy: 12, 17. CC/Wikipedia: front
cover t & c, 1, 9, 11t, 14, 16, 20, 21.

Dewey: 520.9'2
Hardback ISBN 978 1 4451 3058 3
Library eBook ISBN 978 1 4451 3065 1

Printed in China

Franklin Watts is a division of Hachette Children's Books,
an Hachette UK company.

www.hachette.co.uk

Contents

A merchant's son

Nicolaus Copernicus was born in 1473 into a
wealthy family. His father was a merchant and
the family home was often filled with visitors.

The family home in Torun, Poland.

1473–1490

LVCAS ...IALLEN.

His uncle, Lucas Watzenrode, eventually became a bishop.

Copernicus is born, the youngest of four children. His name was originally spelt Niklas Koppernigk.

1480s

He starts at the local church school.

1483

His father dies.

When Copernicus was only ten, his father died. His uncle, Lucas Watzenrode, looked after the family and made sure that Copernicus and his brother had a good education.

To university

In 1491 Copernicus became a student in Krakow. He studied maths and natural sciences, astronomy and poetry. Much of what he learnt dated back to the time of the ancient Greeks.

Krakow, the then-capital city of Poland, as it looked in 1493.

1491–1503

When he visited Rome in 1500, Copernicus was able to observe an eclipse of the Moon.

1491–95

He attends university in Krakow with his brother.

1496

He studies Church law in Bologna.

1500

He gives a lecture on maths in Rome.

1501–03

He studies medicine at the University of Padua.

His studies continued in Italy, where he studied law and then medicine. While he was at the University of Bologna, he lived with a professor of astronomy and helped him study the night sky.

Hardworking star-gazer

1503

Copernicus returns to Poland and works for his uncle.

1508

He starts to form new ideas about how the Universe works.

1509

He translates ancient Greek poems from Latin and publishes them.

1510

He moves to Frombork.

Copernicus lived with his uncle in this castle at Lidzbark.

In 1503 Copernicus returned to Poland to work for his uncle, who was now a bishop. He helped with the business side of his uncle's job and also worked as his doctor.

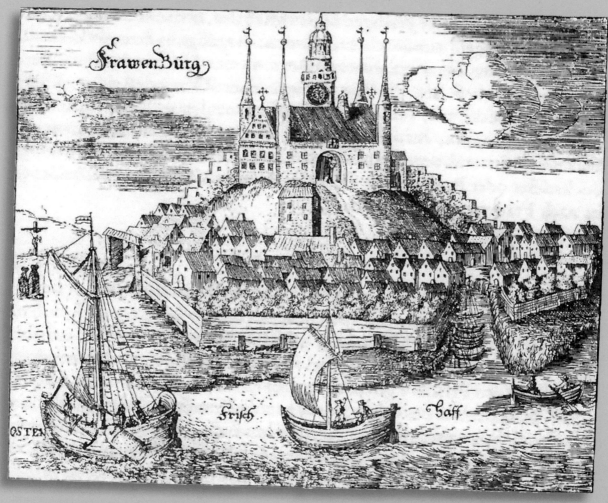

This view of Frombork and its cathedral dates from around 1650.

Most of his spare time was spent studying the night sky and he became well known for his skill. In 1510, he moved to Frombork to help run the cathedral's business affairs.

EXPERIMENT

Like Copernicus, you can study the night sky without a telescope. Find a star map in a book or download one from the Internet (the BBC Stargazing LIVE site is very useful). It will help you find and name stars in the night sky.

9

The old ideas

At this time, most people believed that the Earth was at the centre of the Universe. They saw the Sun rise in the east and set in the west. People in the Catholic Church believed that God had created the world with the Earth at the centre of everything.

This photographer kept his camera in exactly the same place to make this photo showing the path of the Sun across the sky during one day.

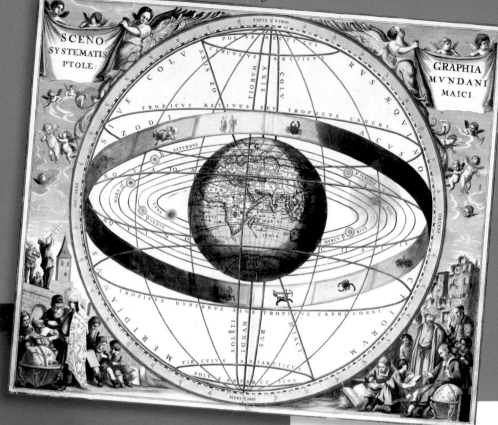

This map, made in 1660, shows Ptolemy's geocentric Universe, with the Earth at the centre.

Students learnt about the work of Greek astronomer, Ptolemy, who died in 141 CE. He placed the Earth at the centre of the Universe with the Sun and the planets revolving around it. He explained the movement of the planets across the night sky by drawing up a complicated system of loops.

Copernicus' new idea

Copernicus made observations of the night sky from one of the towers of Frombork Castle.

Copernicus was sure that there must be a more simple, beautiful answer to how the Universe worked. His ideas placed the Sun at the centre with the Earth and the other planets revolving around it. This was revolutionary.

BREAKTHROUGH

Copernicus worked out that the Earth and the other planets circled around the Sun. He also thought that the Earth rotated on its axis every 24 hours.

1510

Astronomers, and later sailors, used a cross-staff to note the height, or altitude, of stars in the night sky.

Astronomers used scientific instruments including the cross-staff, the quadrant, the triquetrum and the armillary sphere. Copernicus used them to make detailed maps of the stars and the movement of the Moon and the planets across the night sky.

1510

Copernicus writes his ideas down in a handwritten booklet.

13

Maths proves his idea

Copernicus worked out that the further the distance between a planet and the Sun, the longer it took for it to go around the Sun. The more he worked on the maths and his observations of the night sky, the more he was sure he was right. He let a few friends look at a written outline of his ideas.

In 1660, this illustration of Copernicus' idea, called the heliocentric model, was printed in a book of maps.

1510 onwards

Copernicus lets a few friends look at an outline of his ideas.

1512

His uncle, the bishop, dies.

1513

Copernicus has a flat area built in his garden for his scientific instruments.

BREAKTHROUGH

Copernicus worked out the correct order of the planets in orbit around the Sun.

Working for the Church

All this time, Copernicus continued to work for the Catholic Church. He helped to run Church estates, collected rents and settled arguments. He continued this work in Olsztyn when he moved there in 1516, and even organised the defence of the castle during a war.

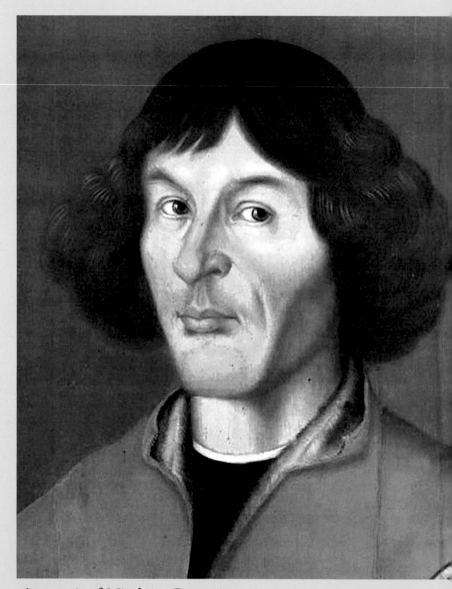

A portrait of Nicolaus Copernicus.

1513

Copernicus sends his ideas on how to make the calendar more accurate to churchmen in Rome, the centre of the Catholic Church.

1516–21

He moves to Olsztyn. He works on ideas for reforming the coinage of Poland.

Although busy with his job, he found time to draw a huge sundial on one wall of the castle where he lived. He used it to collect details of the movement of the Sun across the sky during the year, to help measure the true length of a year.

Copernicus lived in these rooms in Olsztyn Castle.

On the Revolutions

1520s

Across Europe, people are talking about Martin Luther's attacks on the Catholic Church.

1522 onwards

Copernicus returns to live in Frombork. His close friends encourage him to publish his ideas.

In this engraving, Copernicus holds a plant that shows he is a doctor.

When he was alone, Copernicus was writing down more and more calculations that proved his ideas about the Universe. This took him over twenty years but by around 1530 he had gathered everything together in a book called *On the Revolutions*.

Non parem Pauli gratiam requiro
Veniam Petri neq, posco, sed quam
In cruces ligno dederas latroni
sedulus oro.

However he did not publish his book. He was afraid of what powerful people in the Church might say since most people in the Church believed that God had put Earth at the centre of the Universe. He also thought people would make fun of him.

Copernicus kept his Christian beliefs and did not want to be thrown out of the Catholic Church.

19

Rheticus arrives

Now in his sixties, Copernicus felt quite lonely when some of his closest friends moved away. All this changed with the arrival of a young student called Rheticus. He hoped to persuade Copernicus to publish *On the Revolutions*.

This picture shows the title page of Rheticus' book on triangles, printed in 1551.

1538-1542

For months, Rheticus helped Copernicus correct and prepare the book for publication. He even took the manuscript, section by section, to the best printer in Germany.

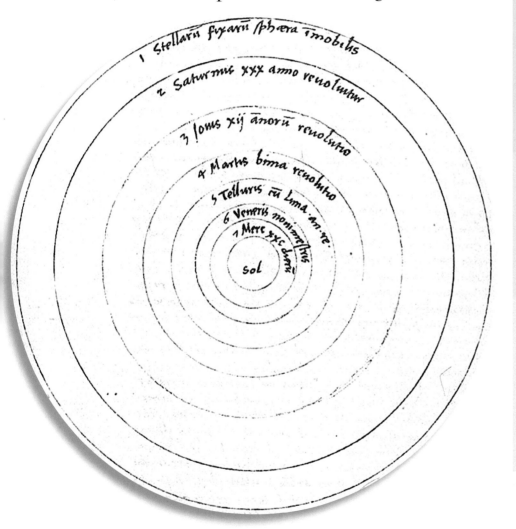

The book, On the Revolutions of the Heavenly Spheres, *contained this diagram to explain Copernicus' ideas.*

1538

Close friends leave Frombork.

1539

He is forced to make his housekeeper leave, on the orders of the bishop.

1539

Rheticus comes to stay.

1540

A short version of Copernicus' ideas is published.

Nov/Dec 1542

Copernicus has a stroke.

Death and beyond

A printed copy of *On the Revolutions of the Heavenly Spheres* reached Copernicus as he lay dying in May 1543. As Copernicus had feared, over time many people in the Church began to hate his ideas. In 1616, the Church banned his book.

It is said that Copernicus held a printed copy of his book as he died.

1543	**24 May 1543**	**16th and 17th centuries**	**1616**
On the Revolutions of the Heavenly Spheres is published with this longer title.	Copernicus dies and is buried in Frombork Cathedral.	His work inspires other great scientists.	The Church bans Copernicus' book – no one prints new copies.

1543 to now

In May 2010, Copernicus' bones were reburied in Frombork Cathedral with a grand funeral service.

Despite this, scientists and scholars in the 16th and 17th centuries continued to read his book. Today he is recognised as one of the world's most important scientists, who placed the Earth and the planets in their correct positions around the Sun.

1835	1945	1972	2000s	2010
The Church's ban on the book is lifted.	Nicolaus Copernicus University opens in Torun, Poland.	A crater on the Moon is named after him.	People search for Copernicus' bones under the floor of Frombork Cathedral.	Copernicus is reburied in Frombork Cathedral.

Glossary

armillary sphere A scientific instrument made up of several rings representing the position of planets and stars in the night sky, and used to measure their positions.

astronomer An expert who studies stars, planets and outer space.

axis Here, the imaginary line that passes straight through the spinning planet, Earth.

bishop A priest who has power in the Church over other priests.

coinage The coins of different values used by a country.

heliocentric The Sun (known as *helios* in Greek) at the centre, with the planets rotating around it.

Martin Luther (1483–1546) A German monk whose ideas and writings inspired a movement for change, and the formation of the Protestant Church.

merchant Someone who buys and sells things in large quantities.

natural sciences The study of biology, chemistry and physics.

observations Taking note and recording what you see.

orbit The path that a planet takes around the Sun.

quadrant A maths instrument used to measure the height of stars in the sky.

revolution One complete turn of an object that is rotating.

sphere An object shaped like a ball.

stroke A serious illness that often leaves people paralysed.

sundial An instrument used to tell the time.

triquetrum A maths instrument used to measure the position of the stars in the sky.

Universe Everything that is known to exist – our galaxy and all the others but in Copernicus' time, it meant the Sun and the planets that orbited it.

Index